D1442567

Sasha & Malia Obama

ABDO
Publishing Company

A Big Buddy Book
by **Sarah Tieck**

VISIT US AT
www.abdopublishing.com

Published by ABDO Publishing Company, 8000 West 78th Street, Edina, Minnesota 55439.

Copyright © 2010 by Abdo Consulting Group, Inc. International copyrights reserved in all countries. No part of this book may be reproduced in any form without written permission from the publisher. Buddy Books™ is a trademark and logo of ABDO Publishing Company.

Printed in the United States of America, North Mankato, Minnesota.

Coordinating Series Editor: Rochelle Baltzer
Contributing Editors: Megan M. Gunderson, BreAnn Rumsch, Marcia Zappa
Graphic Design: Maria Hosley
Cover Photograph: *AP Photo*: Ron Edmonds
Interior Photographs/Illustrations: *AP Photo*: AP Photo (p. 5), AP Photo/File (p. 23), J. Scott Applewhite (p. 25), Chris Carlson (p. 11), Vandell Cobb/Ebony Collection via AP Images (p. 7), Jim Cole (p. 11), Charles Dharapak (p. 23), Ron Edmonds (pp. 5, 15, 23, 27), Ron Edmonds/File (p. 26), Jae C. Hong (p. 12), Chuck Kennedy/Pool (p. 19), Peter Kramer (p. 24), Jose Luis Magana (p. 15), Yeoman 1st Class Donna Lou Morgan/Department of Defense (p. 21), Charlie Neibergau/File (p. 20), John Rous (p. 25), Callie Shell/Obama Transition Office (p. 17), Evan Vucci (p. 29); *Getty Images*: Chris Ommanney (p. 9).

Library of Congress Cataloging-in-Publication Data

Tieck, Sarah, 1976-
  Sasha & Malia Obama : historic first kids / Sarah Tieck.
    p. cm. -- (Big buddy biographies)
  ISBN 978-1-60453-710-9
  1. Obama, Sasha, 2001---Juvenile literature. 2. Obama, Malia, 1998---Juvenile literature. 3. Children of presidents--United States--Biography--Juvenile literature. 4. Obama, Barack--Family--Juvenile literature. I. Title. II. Title: Sasha and Malia Obama.

  E909.O25T54 2010
  973.932092--dc22
  [B]

                              2009009986

  012010
  022010

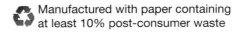 Manufactured with paper containing at least 10% post-consumer waste

Contents

First Daughters

Sasha and Malia Obama are the daughters of President Barack Obama and First Lady Michelle Obama. The Obamas are the first African-American First Family. And, Sasha is the youngest child to live in the White House since the 1960s.

When they moved into the White House, Sasha was seven and Malia was ten. President John F. Kennedy's children were even younger when they moved there in 1961. Caroline was three years old, and John Jr. was just a baby!

Wisconsin

Michigan

LAKE MICHIGAN

Chicago

Iowa

Illinois

Missouri

Indiana

Kentucky

Family Ties

Sasha and Malia are sisters. Natasha "Sasha" Obama was born in 2001. Older sister Malia Obama was born in 1998. Their parents are Barack Jr. and Michelle Obama.

Sasha and Malia were both born in Chicago, Illinois. They were raised in a part of the city called Hyde Park-Kenwood. Michelle's mother, Marian Shields Robinson, lived nearby.

Sasha and Malia's parents met in Chicago in 1989. They got married in 1992.

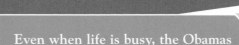

Even when life is busy, the Obamas find time to spend together.

Sasha and Malia grew up in a working family. Their mom and dad both worked as lawyers and in community-based jobs. Later, their dad wrote books and became an Illinois state senator.

As Barack became more well known, Sasha and Malia's lives changed. People recognized the Obama girls and took pictures of them.

Campaign Trail

Sasha and Malia's dad wanted to be the president of the United States. The president is the head of the U.S. government. This is a very important job!

In February 2007, Barack started his campaign. This was a busy time for the Obamas. Sometimes, the entire family traveled. Other times, Sasha and Malia stayed home with their grandma Marian.

Senator Joe Biden ran for vice president with Barack. Sasha and Malia became friends with Joe's grandchildren. They even had a sleepover during the campaign.

As part of his campaign, Barack traveled all over the United States. He gave speeches and met many people.

FOR OBAMA

Did you know...

In July 2008, Malia celebrated her tenth birthday on the campaign trail. The Obamas ordered takeout in their hotel room in Montana. Then they danced to Malia's favorite songs.

Sasha and Malia spent most of election night in a hotel room with their parents. There, they watched the news as the votes were counted.

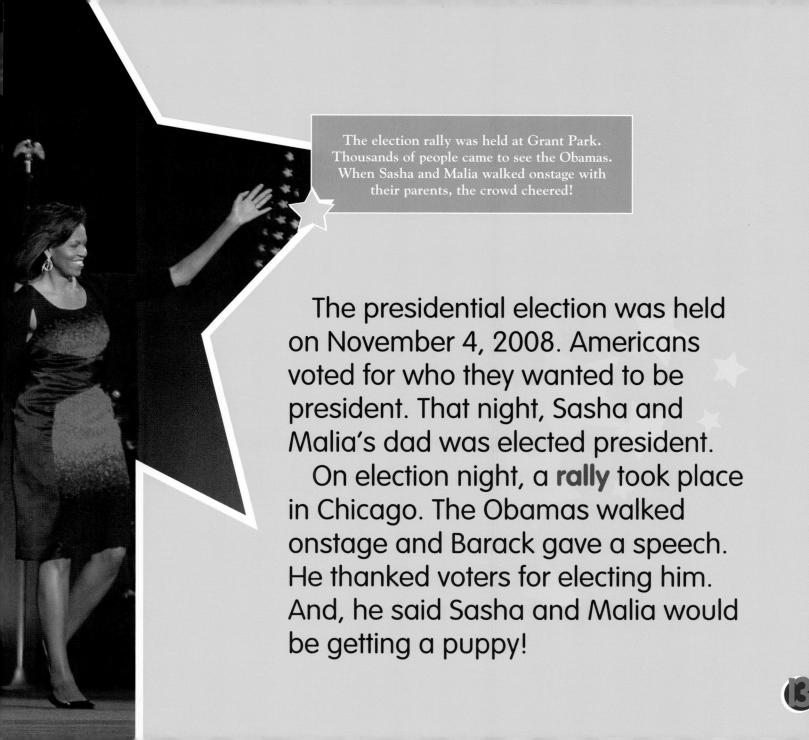

The election rally was held at Grant Park. Thousands of people came to see the Obamas. When Sasha and Malia walked onstage with their parents, the crowd cheered!

The presidential election was held on November 4, 2008. Americans voted for who they wanted to be president. That night, Sasha and Malia's dad was elected president.

On election night, a **rally** took place in Chicago. The Obamas walked onstage and Barack gave a speech. He thanked voters for electing him. And, he said Sasha and Malia would be getting a puppy!

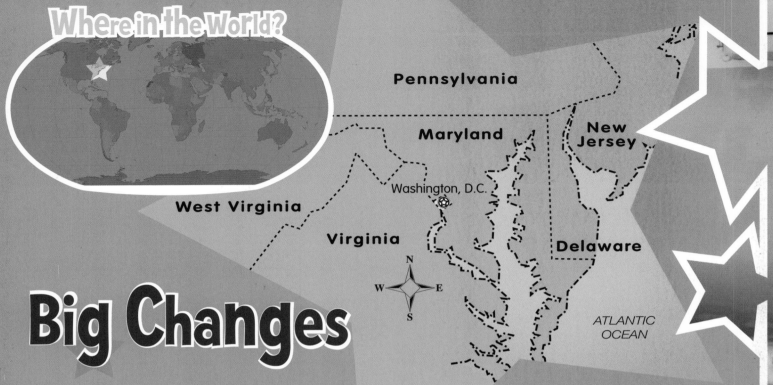

Pennsylvania

Maryland

New Jersey

West Virginia

Washington, D.C.

Virginia

Delaware

N W E S

ATLANTIC OCEAN

Big Changes

Because of Barack's new job, the Obamas moved to Washington, D.C., in January 2009. At that time, Sasha and Malia started attending a new school. They also began making new friends.

Sasha and Malia became famous. They often appeared in magazines and on television. Still, their parents wanted them to have ordinary, quiet lives.

The military and guards called Secret Service agents often travel with the First Family. They make sure the First Family is safe.

SEAL OF THE PRESIDENT OF THE UNITED STATES

Sasha and Malia's grandma Marian also moved to Washington, D.C. Few presidential families have had a live-in grandmother at the White House.

A New School

Sasha and Malia enjoy school. In Chicago, they both attended the University of Chicago Laboratory School. When they moved to Washington, D.C., they started attending Sidwell Friends School. Vice President Joe Biden's grandchildren are students there, too.

Michelle took Sasha and Malia to Sidwell Friends on their first day. They rode in a line of cars with police and Secret Service agents. This is called a motorcade.

Sasha and Malia dressed up in special new clothes for the inauguration. They stood close by to hear their dad say the oath of office. He swore the oath with one hand on a Bible, which Michelle held.

Inauguration Day

On January 20, 2009, Barack Obama became the forty-fourth president of the United States. People around the world watched his **inauguration** on television. More than 1 million people were in Washington, D.C., to see it!

Did you know...

Sasha and Malia's dad had a special piece of history at his inauguration. He used the same Bible that Abraham Lincoln had used when he took office in 1861.

On inauguration night, Barack and Michelle dressed up and attended several balls.

While the Obamas were at the inauguration, their belongings were being moved. That night would be their first in the White House.

Sasha and Malia had friends over on inauguration night. They watched movies and had a scavenger hunt. At the end, they opened a door to find the band Jonas Brothers! Sasha and Malia were excited to meet Nick, Joe, and Kevin Jonas.

Did you know...

The White House scavenger hunt helped Sasha and Malia learn about the history of their new home.

People celebrated Barack's inauguration with many events and parties. There were even events for kids!

The White House

The president's family lives in the White House. There are more than 100 rooms! These include a movie theater, a pool, and a bowling alley.

The White House has changed over the years. Construction started in 1792. Most presidents have lived there with their families. Government offices are located there, too.

At one time, the Lincoln Bedroom was President Abraham Lincoln's office. Malia hoped doing her homework at his desk would inspire her to have big thoughts.

The White House is located at 1600 Pennsylvania Avenue in Washington, D.C.

Barack surprised Sasha and Malia with a brand-new swing set! It is on the White House lawn.

Presidential Kids

Over the years, many children have lived in the White House. The most recent First Kids, Barbara Bush and Jenna Hager, wrote a letter to Sasha and Malia. It was printed in the *Wall Street Journal*. It gave Sasha and Malia advice on being the president's daughters.

Did you know...

The Secret Service has code names for Sasha and Malia. Sasha's is Rosebud. Malia's is Radiance.

Chelsea Clinton is President Bill Clinton's only child. She attended Sidwell Friends, like Sasha and Malia.

Julie Nixon Eisenhower and Tricia Nixon Cox are President Richard Nixon's daughters. Tricia (*right*) got married at the White House on June 12, 1971.

25

Michelle believes healthy eating is important. So, the Obamas planted a garden at the White House. They plan to grow vegetables, herbs, and berries.

Daily Life

Even though the White House has a staff, Sasha and Malia still do chores. Every day they make their beds, pick up their rooms, and do their homework. They each get one dollar for a weekly **allowance**.

The girls also take care of their puppy. In April 2009, they got a Portuguese water dog and named him Bo. He was a reward for their help during the campaign.

Bo was six months old when Sasha and Malia got him. He was a gift from Senator Edward Kennedy.

Did you know...

The Obama girls are big fans of the Harry Potter books. They even got invited to tour the set of the Harry Potter movies!

Buzz

Since their dad became president, Sasha and Malia have become famous. Many people are interested in their lives. Some even call them **role models**. People are excited to see what is next for Sasha and Malia Obama!

Since the inauguration, life has become very different for the Obamas. But, they still make sure to spend time together as a family.

Did you know...

Sasha and Malia have met *Hannah Montana* star Miley Cyrus. They want to invite her over to watch *Hannah Montana: The Movie.*

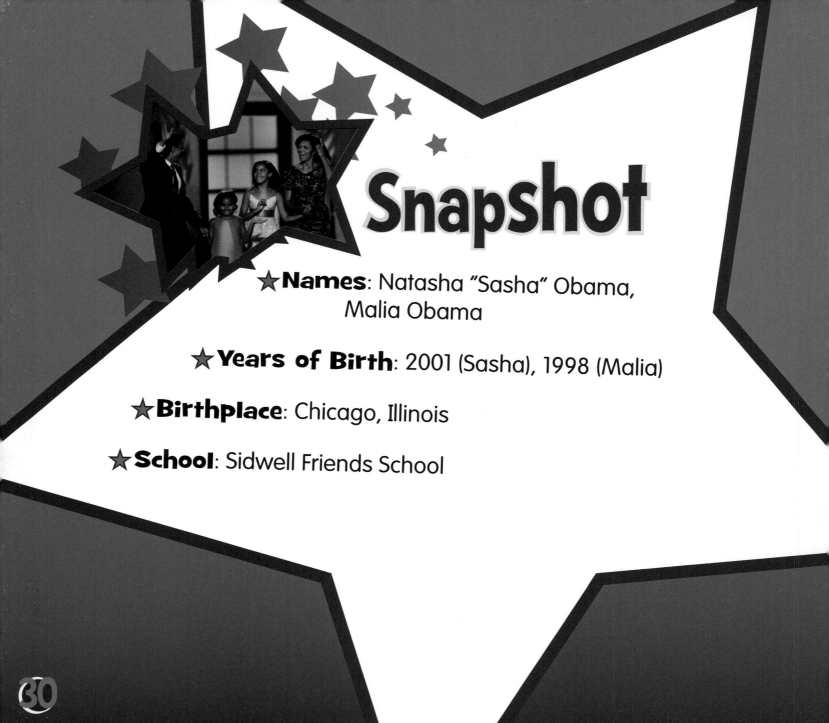

Snapshot

★**Names**: Natasha "Sasha" Obama, Malia Obama

★**Years of Birth**: 2001 (Sasha), 1998 (Malia)

★**Birthplace**: Chicago, Illinois

★**School**: Sidwell Friends School

Important Words

allowance an amount of money regularly paid to a child, especially for doing work around the house.

inauguration (ih-naw-gyuh-RAY-shuhn) a ceremony in which a person is sworn into office.

lawyer a person who gives people advice on laws or represents them in court.

rally an event during which people come together for a common purpose.

role model a person who other people respect and try to act like.

scavenger (SKA-vuhn-juhr) **hunt** an activity during which a person or a group of people search for certain items.

Web Sites

To learn more about Sasha and Malia Obama, visit ABDO Publishing Company online. Web sites about Sasha and Malia Obama are featured on our Book Links page. These links are routinely monitored and updated to provide the most current information available.

www.abdopublishing.com

Index